To:

_____

From: *Venezuela*

_____

Date: 11-5-24.

_____

PRAISE FOR DESERT TO DAWN

"Desert to Dawn is a timely gift poised to inspire, nourish, and empower you to grow and connect with our loving Creator. Catherine's voice will uniquely settle your soul while igniting your spirit."
~Harold G. Koenig, M.D.,
Duke University, Professor of Psychiatry and Behavioral Sciences

*"Catherine Farley has beautifully wrapped her past personal struggles into this marvelous book. Through her faithful connection with God, she guides you from your own desert to dawn and shares wisdom and opportunity for deep reflection.
I pray that your forty-day journey will refresh your mind, body, soul, and spirit."*
~Elza Spaedy, Author of Freedom Through Christ
and Founder of Healed and Restored

"God meets us in the desert. This is what Catherine Farley discovered when she went through a deeply painful chapter in her life. She emerged to write a book to companion others who are lost or spiritually parched as well as anyone who yearns to drink from the wellspring of faith, hope and love. Her vocation as a physical therapist provides a unique perspective and valuable insight. With forty devotions in all, plus exercises, consider Desert to Dawn a retreat for the soul from which you will return refreshed, renewed and truly transformed."
~Julie Marr, Spiritual Director

"With each turn of the page, you'll receive a gift- a gift that leads to stillness and connection to God. Catherine Farley has poured out blessings to those on the journey of faith and integration of heart, mind, soul and spirit. Your soul and heart will be filled with the reflections, images, scripture and prayers."
-Jenny Beaumont, Spiritual Director, Life Coach, Retreat Leader, and Author

DESERT TO DAWN

Reflections to Inspire, Refresh & Renew

Catherine Goodman Farley
with Artist Julie Barnett

DESERT TO DAWN

The information in this book is not intended as a substitute for medical advice. The reader should consult the appropriate medical provider for matters relating to his/her health and particularly with respect to any symptoms that may require diagnosis or medical attention.

Published by Creative Sole, LLC, Charlotte, North Carolina

ISBN:

9780578344461

Edited by Kathy Brown

Design by Kim Hall

Art by Julie Barnett

Photography by Maureen Osborne

Scripture quotes from the Holy Bible, New International Version.

To my husband, Trey, and my children, Madeline, Mary Catherine, and James. Your unconditional love is a gift. May you continue to courageously share it in all you encounter.

CONTENTS

The most beautiful people are those who have known defeat, known suffering, known struggle, known loss, and have found their way out of the depths. These persons have an appreciation, a sensitivity, and an understanding of life that fills them with compassion, gentleness, and a deep loving concern. Beautiful people do not just happen.

~Elisabeth Kubler-Ross

FOREWORD

"You came near when I called you, and you said, 'Do not fear.'"
—Lamentations 3:57

In my early forties, I encountered unexpected and significant loss that shook me to my core. The sudden cardiac death of a dear friend, the life-altering adversity my husband and I faced with a family business financial crisis, and the trauma associated with the loss of three pregnancies created a perfect storm. Our earthly hopes, dreams, and subsequent plans had been ripped to shreds, and I held an uncomfortable uncertainty laced with deep fear. How could we move forward and recover?

I struggled attempting to wrap my logical and scientific mind around the events that had unfolded. As my mind swirled, so followed my body, and I found myself in a state of unrelenting anxiety and panic that ultimately landed me with the dreaded diagnosis of PTSD. Living in a state of fight or flight had become my rhythm, which was not desired, nor sustainable. How could someone who believed in "mind over matter moving you forward" be stuck? As a physical therapist, I was trained in identifying problems, setting forth a plan, and working toward a plausible outcome.

My role had suddenly changed as I lay bed-bound one beautiful summer day with tears emerging from my broken mind and body. The deep unprocessed grief, pain, and worry paralyzed me. There was no plan, just stillness and suffering. Providentially and thankfully, I sensed that I had been lovingly cracked open for a purpose. My faith was being radically tested. I could not control what had happened, nor could I see far enough ahead to recognize what the outcome might be. The only option was to truly surrender and allow God to do the work that He intended to do in this season of my life. He was replacing the fear and chaos in my soul with His peace and presence, and I needed to let go.

Through struggles and successes, I discovered a wide array of therapeutic tools and fresh rhythms that would eventually set me free. Ultimately, I trusted and let go of chaos that I could not control. My eyes were drawn to the inspiration found in nature, my heart was opened to the earthly angels surrounding me, and my hands were gifted with the pen to write. God planted new seeds in the cracks and crevices, and taught me how to better nourish my soul through a deeper connection with His Spirit. He was providing space for inspiration, discovery, and growth. I simply needed to be open.

As I write this guided devotional almost ten years later, I am awed by the work He has accomplished in little old me. He has offered me a lens to notice when a twinge of anxiety is percolating and has protected me from the deep pangs that PTSD might bring. The long nights of trying to rest with panic and a racing heart are gone. God truly qualifies the unqualified and brings purpose from our pain.

INTRODUCTION

You have come to these pages for a variety of reasons, from a range of experiences with diverse paths. Our world in all of its glory holds real stressors, traumatic experiences, and situations filled with emotional upheaval. Amid these times, our Creator does allow challenges to befall us, but He promises to walk with us. I assert that it is in these very times that He is closest to us and is doing His most glorious work. Often, our toughest seasons are the catalyst for breathtaking growth and beauty. Through our belief in God and the faith we possess, hope always prevails.

The merging of faith and science in this unique guided devotional is the foundation for reflective work that will move you to the discovery of your deeper self. Grounded in the beliefs that our Creator is our providential physician and that our bodies are a dwelling place for the Holy Spirit, the prompts will provide a framework for inspiration, discovery, and growth. The scientific assertion of neuroplasticity affirms the intricate connection between the mind and the body. Our mindset largely impacts the function of the body; likewise, the sensory input received by the body affects our mind. With this triad of factors in play, these daily reflections will provide sound spiritual guidance interwoven with mind and body science to provide fruitful growth.

Prior to your forty-day journey of inspiration, prayer, and reflection, you will have the opportunity to discover some beautiful rhythms that may enhance your spiritual growth. You may be drawn to create a sacred space, begin guided meditation or progressive relaxation, or try journaling gratitude. Whatever rhythm resonates with you, I encourage you to weave it into your day and discover the amazing impact.

Setting aside time for stillness and reflection with your Creator can foster tremendous peace and love. These are gifts that God wants to give you in abundance. Be present to these pages and to what speaks to you. The Holy Spirit is alive and ready to guide and nourish. Remember, you were uniquely created to thrive.

NOTICING GOD IN CREATION AND ART

"But ask the animals, and they will teach you, or the birds in the sky,
and they will tell you, or speak to the earth, and it will teach you,
or let the fish in the sea inform you."
—Job 12:7–8

Before God created the human mind, body, soul, and spirit, He attended to the glorious surroundings of nature that would support and nourish us as humans. Our Creator had intricate plans in the heavens and the earth, the sea and the sky, the plants and the animals, and every little thing in between.

The peace and presence of God floods the senses when we can spend time and notice His beautiful ways in our natural surroundings. As you turn the pages of this guided devotional, we hope that you will see the glorious reflection of God's creation. The art, combined with inspiring words and questions to ponder, are intended to open your mind, body, soul, and spirit to your Creator and the potential that is within you. By noticing His imagination, your thoughts will soar to new possibilities as you refresh and renew your perspective of who you are as a beloved child of God.

It is our prayer-filled hope that this journey will touch your senses on many levels and bring about a peace, love, and joy that our Creator intends for each of us. May you be assured that any moments you have spent in the desert are intended to transform you for a new dawn—a dawn that rises each and every day.

Julie Barnett   *Catherine Farley*

Let the morning bring me word of your unfailing love, for I have put my trust in you. Show me the way I should go, for to you I entrust my life. . . . Teach me to do your will, for you are my God; may your good Spirit lead me on level ground.

—Psalm 143:8, 10

CREATING YOUR SACRED SPACE

As you embark upon this forty-day journey, I encourage you to set the scene for your reading and reflecting. Our surroundings have a tremendous impact upon our minds and bodies. In creating your sacred space, consider what may make you feel at ease and allow your mind to be open. If you want peace, surround yourself with reminders of peace. If you need energy, create a stimulating environment, and so on.

A FEW CONSIDERATIONS:

Color—soft or vibrant depending upon your needs

Chair—comfortable and supportive

Lighting—dim or bright depending upon your comfort

Privacy—a quiet space

Scents—a candle, flower, or essential oils

An inspiring quote

Pictures of a loved one, a supportive person in your life, or a memorable place

Bring nature indoors or consider an outdoor setting

Choose a consistent time of day

Surround yourself with sacred items that remind you of your faith

Certain springs are tapped only when we are alone. The artist knows he must be alone to create; the writer, to work out his thoughts; the musician, to compose; the saint, to pray. But women need solitude in order to find again the true essence of themselves; that firm strand which will be the indispensable center of a whole web of human relationships. She must find that inner stillness where the mind and the body connect to the soul.

~Anne Morrow Lindbergh

PREPARATION: MIND, BODY, SPIRIT

After setting the scene, notice how your mind and body feel. Are you focused, or is your mind reeling with scattered thoughts? Are you relaxed and open to a new experience, or are you tense and resistant? If you notice restlessness, take the time to settle your mind and body. You may find some of these methods helpful in resetting. Try one at a time and establish a consistent practice so you will know what technique is most beneficial.

MIND

4-7-8 BREATHING EXERCISE FOR RELAXATION AND CALM

1. Sit with your back straight.
2. Place the tip of your tongue against the ridge of the tissue behind your front teeth.
3. Exhale completely through your mouth making a whoosh sound.
4. Close your mouth and inhale through your nose to count of 4.
5. Hold your breath for count of 7.
6. Exhale completely through your mouth making a whoosh sound for a count of 8.
7. Repeat the cycle 3 times.

GUIDED IMAGERY AND VISUALIZATION FOR POSITIVE SENSORY INPUT

1. Sit quietly and comfortably with your eyes closed.
2. Bring to mind a vision that is relaxing.
3. Note the senses you feel with the vision.
4. What do you see? What do you feel? What do you hear? What do you smell? What do you taste?
5. Bring to mind the desired outcomes.

BODY

GROUNDING EXERCISE TO REST IN THE PRESENT MOMENT

1. Acknowledge 5 things you can see.
2. Acknowledge 4 things you can touch.
3. Acknowledge 3 things you can hear.
4. Acknowledge 2 things you can smell.
5. Acknowledge 1 thing you can taste.

OPEN POSTURE

1. Shoulders back and relaxed.
2. Chest open.
3. Palms open and resting in your lap or on arm of chair.
4. Eye gaze slightly upward.
5. Legs hip-width apart.
6. Feet grounded on the floor.

PROGRESSIVE MUSCLE RELAXATION

1. Sit in a comfortable position and close your eyes.
2. Systematically tighten muscles for 5 seconds and then release, repeating twice for each muscle group.
3. Begin with the face, neck, shoulders, back, chest, abdomen, arms, hands, legs, feet, and whole body.
4. Scan the body and repeat for any areas that remain tense.

RELAXATION RESPONSE FOR STRESS REDUCTION

1. Sit quietly in a comfortable position.
2. Close your eyes.
3. Deeply relax all of your muscles, beginning at your feet and progressing up to your face. Keep them relaxed.
4. Breathe through your nose, becoming aware of your breathing. As you breathe out, say the word "one" silently to yourself.
5. Breathe easily and naturally, repeating for 10–20 minutes.
6. When you finish, sit quietly for a few minutes, open your eyes, and rise slowly.

SPIRIT

MEDITATION WITH THE HOLY SPIRIT

1. Sitting comfortably, invite the Holy Spirit to dwell deeply within you.
2. Envision the warmth of the fire of the Holy Spirit illuminating areas that need care, the waters of the Holy Spirit cleansing and purifying, and the winds of the Holy Spirit providing support and energy.
3. Imagine His transformational presence in each of the cells of your body multiplying and filling you with the abundant love from your Creator.
4. Continue to breathe deeply and rest in the comfort knowing that God is at work in your life through the movement of His Spirit.

SCRIPTURE READING AND PROMPTINGS

1. Go to a quiet place to prepare to listen to the Word of God.
2. After listening or reading aloud scripture, pause and recall if some word or phrase stood out or something touched your heart. If so, take a pause and notice the insight or feeling.
3. Read the passage again for fuller meaning. You may also choose to write down the scripture and your reflection. This is one of the many ways that our Creator connects with us.

PRACTICING GRATITUDE

"Give thanks to the Lord, for he is good; his love endures forever."
—1 Chronicles 16:34

Your focus on your gifts brings cause for thanksgiving. A simple practice of acknowledging what you behold instead of what you lack can shift your perspective and lift your spirits even in the most challenging times. Studies show that a practice of gratitude can be the catalyst for improved well-being and health. One of my favorite ways to practice gratitude is to hold my hands in front of me and count on my fingers the many gifts in my life. No matter what is taking place in our lives, we can all find "handfuls" of gratitude. Begin with the air you are breathing and build from there.

Writing gratitude in a journal is also a beautiful and impactful way to notice all of the good in your life. When you establish a practice of jotting down these gifts, you can see the progression over time as thanksgiving builds. Often, a small notebook by your bedside is a wonderful reminder at the end of the day. Writing reinforces this positive mindset and can also aid in your sleep. Give it a try!

Writing is a process in which we discover what lives in us. The writing itself reveals what is alive in us. The deepest satisfaction of writing is precisely that it opens up new spaces within us of which we were not aware before we started to write. To write is to embark upon a journey whose final destination we do not know. Thus, writing requires a real act of trust. We have to say to ourselves, 'I do not yet know what I carry in my heart, but I trust that it will emerge as I write.' Writing is like giving away the few loaves and fishes one has, trusting that they will multiply in the giving. Once we dare to 'give away' on paper a few thoughts that come to us, we start discovering how much is hidden underneath these thoughts. Through it, we gradually come in touch with our own riches.

~Henry Nouwen

WRITING AND REFLECTING

The average human has over 80,000 thoughts each day, and almost 80 percent of those are self-questioning or self-deprecating. Focusing on the negative ruminating thoughts is almost always non-productive and potentially harmful to your well-being. Learning to harness the questions that may prompt reflection and growth can bring about a deeper understanding of who you are and of your beautiful potential. Simply expressing yourself through writing can be life-changing.

Some of the benefits of practicing expressive writing or journaling include improved sleep, decreased anxiety and depression, improved resilience and cognitive functioning, enhanced emotional regulation, decreased blood pressure, and a positive shift in mood, to name a few. Recalling thoughts or worries that are on replay and writing them down can be the first step in letting go of something that is no longer serving you. Simply put, getting your thoughts onto paper is therapeutic.

As you journey from desert to dawn, you will notice the questions to ponder each day. After each section of the forty-day journey, there are writing pages provided. I encourage you to journal your thoughts. Whatever comes to mind, put it on paper. It may be something that needs to be purged, or maybe something you write will bring you clarity. Trust that the process will bring about transformation and growth when you invite the Holy Spirit to guide you. Soon you may find that you have journaled your way to joy!

Very early in the morning, while it was still dark, Jesus got up, left the house and went off to a solitary place, where he prayed.

—Mark 1:35

RHYTHM FOR THE FORTY-DAY JOURNEY

You will be guided through surrender, transformation, integration, and affirmation as you find a peace where deeper purpose and intention can be discovered. As you focus on each ten-day leg of the journey, you will rise to a new level of connection with your Creator, ultimately bringing you freedom from thoughts that no longer serve you.

By surrendering your mind, body, soul, and spirit to your Creator, you will discover the depth of God's unconditional love for you. Fear and doubt will take a back seat and your beautifully unique gifts will be revealed. He will hold you tight. He will lift you. He will plant you in fertile soil so that you will flourish, ultimately giving you the courage to share your beautiful gifts with the world around you.

As you are guided through the next forty days of caring for your mind, body, soul, and spirit, be open, let go, and allow the Spirit of our loving God into the cracks and crevices. You will discover beauty, connection, and calling in these places. Allow Him to transform you into His image and likeness and into the best version of you. Place your trust in His promise: "See, I am doing a new thing! Now it springs up: do you not perceive it? I am making a way in the wilderness and streams in the wasteland" (Isaiah 43:19).

A PRAYER FOR YOUR JOURNEY

Dearest God, my Creator and Friend,
I am walking in the desert right now. Please be with me when the sand is hot and I'm scared to step forward, when the air becomes too dry and I'm breathless, and when the winds make me spin.
Allow your peaceful presence to pervade my mind, body, soul, and spirit. Strengthen and give me courage in this journey. May these forty days guide me through the desert to a new dawn.
In faith, I will journey with you by my side. Amen.

INTRODUCTION TO SURRENDER

"Open my eyes that I may see wonderful things in your law."
—Psalm 119:18

Our openness is a beautiful invitation and opportunity for our Creator to do His most glorious work. You may come to this journey with specific intentions to grow spiritually, or maybe you are in a time of transition seeking inspiration, or you might be traversing a season of tremendous pain and feel as though your heart has been cracked open. God will meet you wherever you are. He will commune with you and guide you to places you could never imagine. Your cracks, no matter how deep and jagged, are the places where He goes to transform your pain into purpose, to bring healing to your hurt, and to fill you with His love and peace. Meeting you in your most vulnerable places, He promises that His "grace is sufficient for you" and that His power is "made perfect" in your weakness (2 Corinthians 12:9).

It can be scary to look inward and notice what is truly present. The grief, the shame, the guilt, and the weighty expectations are heavy, but our gracious and loving God is always ready to lift these burdens. He reassures us in scripture time and time again, as in Matthew 11:29: "Take my yoke upon you and learn from me, for I am gentle and humble in heart, and you will find rest for your souls."

He showers us with His unconditional love and mercy, fostering abundant grace in our lives. Our openness and surrender to His help are not signs of weakness but signs of tremendous strength and courage.

As you journey the next ten days, focus on the word each day and allow God to weave the truth into your mind, body, soul, and spirit. Ponder these questions and place your deepest thoughts, worries, and pains in His healing hands. He is the ultimate physician and can heal every single part of you.

TO PONDER . . .

~Do I have past experiences or unhealed wounds that are holding me back from becoming who God intended me to be?

~What do I hold that can be transformed by God's word and truth?

~Are there people I need to forgive so that my heart can be free from hurt and resentfulness?

A PRAYER FOR SURRENDER

Dearest God, my Creator and Friend,
I am grateful for your gentle nudge to open up to you. Help me to be authentic and allow you into the depths of my being. You created me and you know every cell in my body and the places where I am broken. Help me to grow through my weakness and vulnerability. Allow the hardened places in my heart to soften in your hands. Guide me with your loving care and aid me in the discovery of my beautiful self. May I become a conduit of your love and mercy, radiating your light into the world.
In faith, I will journey with you by my side. Amen.

"For we walk by faith, not by sight."
—2 Corinthians 5:7

The fruit of silence is prayer, the fruit of prayer is faith, the fruit of faith is love, the fruit of love is service, and the fruit of service is peace.

~Saint Mother Teresa

ONE

PRAYER

"Arise, cry out in the night, as the watches of the night begin; pour out your heart like water in the presence of the Lord."

—Lamentations 2:19

Prayer can come in many fashions and forms, but ultimately, it is the way we communicate with our Creator. Exploring the many ways we can pray is a soulful journey. Whether it is through a quiet walk in nature, listening to or singing a heartfelt song, reading scripture, creating art, journaling, or even sitting in silence, you will discover your unique prayer language. I encourage you to give it a try. The peace you will hold in these sacred moments is irreplaceable.

As you begin to discover your prayer rhythm, you will notice that you begin to share your thoughts and feelings more easily with God. When you can speak something, it eases the burden on your mind, body, heart, and spirit. This is the first step in letting go. The lifting up of our thoughts and feelings begins the acknowledgment that you can't do it alone. It is your beautiful invitation to God to walk with you, and when He enters, you are empowered. Soon, the desert becomes a place of gentle conversation and a sacred space to share.

~Recall and reflect on a moment when you have been reminded of God's love.

Dearest God, my Creator and Friend,
I am grateful for the opportunity to grow closer to you through prayer. Please guide me to the places in my mind, body, soul, and spirit that need healing and transformation. Help me to discover new ways to communicate with you and encourage me to share my deepest thoughts, worries, and pains with you in prayer. May I be open to the abundant graces that you share with me each and every day.
In faith, I will journey with you by my side. Amen.

Imagine yourself as a living house. God comes in to rebuild that house. At first, perhaps, you can understand what He is doing. He is getting the drains right and stopping the leaks in the roof and so on; you knew that those jobs needed doing and so you are not surprised. But presently He starts knocking the house about in a way that hurts abominably and does not seem to make sense. What on earth is He up to? The explanation is that He is building quite a different house from the one you thought of—throwing out a new wing here, putting on an extra floor there, running up towers, making courtyards. You thought you were being made into a decent little cottage; but He is building a palace.

He intends to come and live in it Himself.

-C. S. Lewis

TWO

GUIDED

"Do not fear, I will help you."
—Isaiah 41:13

It makes sense that "fear not" is the most repeated phrase in scripture. God knows that as humans we will face fears, but He wants to reassure us that He will meet us in the fear and guide us. In this life we will have suffering, but it is what we do in these challenging times that impacts our spirit. Shifting from trying to control every aspect of our lives can actually be freeing and allow space for God to do beautiful work.

As you become more comfortable sharing your fears with God, He will tame them. Your openness and surrender will give space for Him to fill you with faith, hope, and love. It's a decision that we make day in and day out to trust, but the potential when we relinquish control is awe-inspiring. As we are reminded in Matthew 19:26, "With God, all things are possible."

~What is one fear that I can give to God today?

Dearest God, my Creator and Friend,
I am grateful for your healing hand in my life. Please help me to give my fear to you
and trust that your ways are better than mine. Allow my mind, body, soul, and spirit
to be free from the heavy burden of fear. Guide and empower me as I read your
word and hold onto the truths that you share. May I be open to the ways that you
are working in my life and believe in my unbelievable potential when I rely on you.
In faith, I will journey with you by my side. Amen.

THREE

COURAGE

"For the Spirit God gave us does not make us timid, but gives us power, love, and self-discipline."
—2 Timothy 1:7

Change takes courage. As you open your mind, body, soul, and spirit to the hands of your Creator, transformation will occur. By making an intentional choice to connect with God and pay attention to where He is working in your life, you will begin to see fear replaced with courage. Stepping into each day leaving space in your schedule to talk with Him, taking time to be still and sit with Him, and noticing the ways He is whispering to you will bring you reassurance of His loving presence.

Sometimes our greatest growth is realized in the quietest moments when it seems like nothing is happening. This stillness can feel uncomfortable, but this is the place where your Creator creates unbelievable beauty. When the discomfort bubbles up in your heart and soul, take a moment to breathe. Breathe in courage and breathe out the fear that holds you back from becoming who God intended you to be. Maybe this time in the desert was actually intended to grow you in ways you would never imagine.

~What is one new way that I can connect with God today?

Dearest God, my Creator and Friend,
I am grateful for the courage you have woven into my heart and the new ways that I am connecting with you throughout the day. Please help me to notice your gentle nudges and soft whisper. Guide me as I take small steps and changes to strengthen my relationship with you. May I begin to crave the stillness and peace that you provide and resist the restlessness.
In faith, I will journey with you by my side. Amen.

I've learned that people will forget what you've said,
people will forget what you did, but they will never forget how you made them feel.
-Maya Angelou

FOUR

FORGIVENESS

"Be kind and compassionate to one another,
forgiving each other, just as in Christ God forgave you."
—Ephesians 4:32

Forgiveness takes courage. When we choose to forgive, we are placing a situation or person in God's hands and allowing God to do His miraculous healing work. It doesn't necessarily mean that the situation will be resolved or that the person will apologize. What it does bring is freedom from your pain and hurt. Ultimately, this freedom you experience from forgiveness allows space in your mind, body, soul, and spirit for healing. Continuing to live in the pain of unforgiveness can be harmful and weigh you down with resentfulness and anger. When we allow those emotions to fester inside, there is no space for all of the grace that God wants to give you.

The hope that springs forth from the open space the forgiveness brings will reignite your passion for positivity and potential. Even when you are reminded of the hurt, you can refocus to forgiveness and cover the situation or person with prayer. It becomes an intentional but automatic response over time. These are the cycles of renewal that God can create.

~Who or what situation do I need to forgive?

_____

Dearest God, my Creator and Friend,
I am grateful for the opportunity to live a life grounded in forgiveness—a life that offers your forgiveness and mercy for my sins and allows me to offer that same forgiveness to others. Please help me to be courageous and forgive as often as I need so that my heart can be free of hurt. Guide me in healing from the wounds that have festered over time. May I live a life of freedom with you as my central focus.
In faith, I will journey with you by my side. Amen.

There is a crack in everything. That's how the light gets in.

-Leonard Cohen

FIVE

BROKENNESS

"He gives strength to the weary and increases the power of the weak."
—Isaiah 40:29

At times, the weight of our burdens seems unbearable, and we feel weak and possibly broken. You may feel like you can't take another step forward or that you may collapse under the weight of worry. These times are not usually the ones that make the top of the list for best moments, but they are real. We live in a broken world where sin exists. Often, where we turn in these times can be the catalyst for the "next" moments. Could these "broken" places be entry points for something new and glorious in the hands of your Creator?

Our Creator can equip you to do things that you never imagined. Just when you thought you were unqualified, He will give you the tools to accomplish tremendous things. This is where He does His best work—in the unexpected, in the impossible, and in the unbelievable. His imagination far exceeds our ability to comprehend. Think about His creation in nature and how everything was planned and executed. Take a moment one morning and notice the sunrise. There is radiant light, a boldness of color, and a beautiful uniqueness, but it often depends upon the surrounding circumstances. He can do the same things in our human lives. As we shift our mindset to a posture of being open and believing in the goodness of our Creator, we will believe in possibilities and potential.

~What weakness would you like to surrender to God's loving hands?

Dearest God, my Creator and Friend,
I am grateful for your help when I feel weak and broken. Please help me to rely on you to infuse your loving care into the cracks and crevices in my mind, body, soul, and spirit. Allow me to be hopeful and believe that you can always bring beauty from my brokenness. May I be open to the endless possibilities of your love and mercy in my life.

In faith, I will journey with you by my side. Amen.

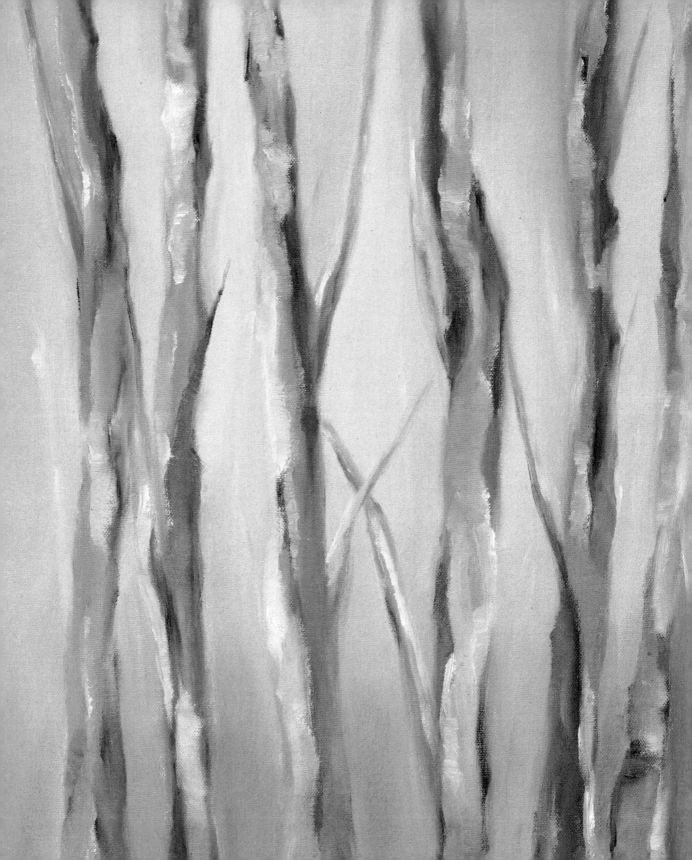

SIX

STILLNESS

"The Lord will fight for you; you need only to be still."
—Exodus 14:14

Our bodies are made for movement, and our lives often reflect all of the many ways that we can move. So where does stillness fit into the picture? Reflecting on God's movement in creation, we understand that He rested on the seventh day. We can also recall times when even Jesus took time to rest. Might stillness be a place where the movement of God can occur in beautiful ways?

When we are still, we can more easily notice what is going on in our bodies. Our heartbeat, our breath, and the flow of our thoughts become more pronounced in stillness. Could these be places that our Creator reaches us and prompts us to notice His loving care for us? Fathers want to spend time with their children. Give Him the opportunity to care for you. He loves you more deeply than you can imagine.

~What is one way you can incorporate stillness with your Creator into your day?

Dearest God, my Creator and Friend,
I am grateful for your constant care and love for me. Please help me to slow down to notice the ways that you are connecting with me in my heart, my mind, my body, and my soul. Guide me as I go through each moment and unite your Spirit with my breath. May I breathe in your peace and comfort and let go of anxiety and worry.
In faith, I will journey with you by my side. Amen.

Allow your pain to become your prayer.

~Father Mike Schmitz

SEVEN

STRENGTH

"I can do all this through him who gives me strength."
—Philippians 4:13

Life can be tough, and the old adage that "God doesn't give you more than you can handle" seems to weigh heavy during our challenging times. Often the trick to walking through these intensely challenging seasons is our reliance and trust in our Creator. He knows us intimately. Imagine the care He took in forming each and every cell in your body. He knows our natural strengths and where we are weak. Could it be that our Creator uses our toughest seasons to grow us in ways unimaginable?

Connecting with our Creator consistently could be the key to unlocking your strength potential. Sometimes, simply looking up to the heavens, a glance to call Him into the moment, takes all of the strength you can muster. Other days, you may find more space to converse with Him. Communicating with your Creator will foster the trust needed to follow His promptings. As we learn how He speaks to us through His gentle whisper and positive promptings, we begin to yearn for this connection. Slowly, you will notice that you crave communion with Him, and you begin to develop a rhythm in your day so that these moments are possible.

~Can you recall a time where an obstacle you encountered ultimately became an opening in your life and an opportunity for growth?

Dearest God, my Creator and Friend,
I am grateful for the strength that you provide me when I can't muster it on my own. Help me to surrender my concerns to your loving hands and trust that your work in my life is so much better than what I can do on my own. I know that you commune with me in a beautifully unique way made just for me. May I notice the many ways that you are connecting with me and embrace new rhythms for sustaining our relationship.

In faith, I will journey with you by my side. Amen.

Sometimes in order to find your voice, you have to step out into unknown territory.

-Allison Fallon

EIGHT

HELD

"Have I not commanded you? Be strong and courageous. Do not be afraid; do not be discouraged, for the Lord your God will be with you wherever you go."
—Joshua 1:9

Uncertainty can be unsettling and may stir up feelings of doubt, but our Creator calls us to trust that He is at work at all times. When fear and doubt are swirling in your mind, body, soul, and spirit, it is difficult to see possibilities and potential. The stirring can sometimes create chaos that is difficult to break through, and it can blur our vision and clarity. Could it be that wrestling and restlessness in your life are moments in which your Creator is "stirring up" something new? Often, He is doing tremendous work in the backdrop of the chaos and confusion.

In uncertain seasons, rekindling our faith and trust takes daily intention. Our rhythms in these times are so important, as we need the structure and routine to combat the external chaos. Establishing a time for stillness with scripture, relaxation, and envisioning being held in your Creator's arms, as well as choosing to surround yourself with positive affirmations and people, are intentional ways to navigate tough seasons. Deciding to focus on the positive and uplifting in spite of the chaos can bring hope and peace. Before you know it, the uncertainty has dissipated, and your mind, body, heart, and soul are unscathed despite the difficulties you have endured. Ultimately, they have been strengthened in the hands of our Creator.

～What is one new rhythm or routine you can establish to ground you in God's loving arms?

Dearest God, my Creator and Friend,
I am grateful for the strength and courage you provide me in times of uncertainty. I know you desire to hold me and even carry me through challenging seasons. Please help me to surrender to you and to choose healthy rhythms and routines that will restore and not destroy my mind, body, soul, and spirit. May I trust in the difficult times that I can let go and be open to your plans for my life.
In faith, I will journey with you by my side. Amen.

NINE

COMPASSION

"Let us then approach God's throne of grace with confidence, so that we may receive mercy and find grace to help us in our time of need."
—Hebrews 4:16

The grace of our Creator moves us toward compassion for ourselves and others. Having compassion with ourselves is a beautiful first step to accepting our weaknesses and limitations and in understanding that God's grace can renew us. As we grow in compassion for ourselves, boundaries are broken. The grace and compassion that have broken free can now be shared with others, yielding fellowship and community. Could it be that our brokenness may be the catalyst for self-renewal that will ultimately impact the lives of others?

As this beauty of openness becomes a ritual in your life, you become a conduit of all that our Creator desires to share with His creation. The outflowing of love, mercy, and compassion is endless when we maintain a focus toward our gentle Creator. Imagine the ripple effect in a community where this abundance is available to all. Needs are filled, love is shared, and God's grace is always present and noticed. The catalyst for massive renewal occurs one step at a time, and it can begin at any moment you choose.

~What grace and compassion can I give myself today?

Dearest God, my Creator and Friend,
I am grateful for the grace and compassion that you have bestowed upon me.
Please help me to be gentle with myself and allow your grace to flood upon my
worries and broken places. Allow me to see your gentle touches in my life, bringing
about compassion. May I be a beautiful conduit for the compassion, love, and mercy
that I receive in abundance from you.
In faith, I will journey with you by my side. Amen.

The Serenity Prayer

God grant me the serenity to accept the things I cannot change, the courage to change the things I can, and the wisdom to know the difference.

TEN

FAITH

"'For I know the plans I have for you,' declares the Lord, 'plans to prosper you and not to harm you, plans to give you hope and a future. Then you will call on me and come and pray to me, and I will listen to you. You will seek me and find me when you seek me with all your heart.'"
—Jeremiah 29:11–13

Faith provides the foundation and perspective for a life grounded in hope. When we face challenges or seasons of suffering, our faith allows us to continue to experience joy because we understand that our Creator is with us. With this mindset, our joy and suffering, beauty and brokenness can coexist. The intertwining of these seemingly contradicting states actually yields tremendous resiliency. As we reframe situations from a hopeful perspective, we see light instead of darkness, and we notice possibilities in lieu of obstacles. Ultimately, a faith-filled mind replaces the swirling doubt and anxiety that can exist.

As you let go of negative thought patterns and begin to feed your mind with positive affirmations, peace and calm have a place to rest. The open space in your mind can be filled with the truth of who you are and who you were meant to be. Simply, you are a beloved and uniquely created child of God. He made you in His image and likeness. He created you to thrive in His loving care. Repeating these affirmations will slowly bring belief and constant awareness of His loving presence in your life. Allow this thought to settle deeply into your mind, body, soul, and spirit.

~What positive affirmation of who you are as a child of God can you embrace?

Dearest God, my Creator and Friend,
I am grateful for the tremendous gift of faith you have given me. Please help me to believe to the depths of my soul that I am a beautiful child of yours created to thrive. Help me to hold to hope in my joy and in my pain and give me perspective of the beauty you see in me. May these healthy new rhythms pervade my mind, body, soul, and spirit as I am transformed in your unconditional love.
In faith, I will journey with you by my side. Amen.

THOUGHTS

TO PONDER

INTRODUCTION TO TRANSFORMATION

"I will give you a new heart and put a new spirit within you; I will remove the heart of stone and give you a heart of flesh."
—Ezekiel 36:26

As you notice the open space within your mind, body, and soul, invite the Spirit of our Creator to dwell within you. It is in this space that the movement of the Spirit will squelch fear and anxiety, reigniting hope and possibility. Scripture instructs us in Philippians 4:6-7: "Do not be anxious about anything, but in every situation, by prayer and petition, with thanksgiving, present your requests to God. And the peace of God, which transcends all understanding, will guard your hearts and your minds in Christ Jesus." Rest assured, your wounds and pain will be transformed into wisdom and understanding. Offering them up to our Creator allows you the freedom to move through each moment and every single day in hopeful trust.

When moments of restlessness present, acknowledge the stirring and continue to invite the Spirit to reside within you. This may be a moment that you need to pause, breathe deeply, and reflect upon the good. As Ralph Waldo Emerson shared, "Sometimes we must adopt the pace of nature, whose secret is patience." As you focus upon the good with patience, your thoughts will follow, and your perspective will shift. Over time, the repetition of this invitation becomes a new rhythm that yields a beautiful awareness and connection to the loving presence of our Creator. Come, Holy Spirit.

As you journey the next ten days, focus on the word and scripture each day, inviting God to weave His truth into your mind, body, soul, and spirit. Ponder these questions and allow His Spirit to guide your hope-filled thoughts. He will take you to places you never imagined.

TO PONDER . . .

~ What weakness or challenge could I surrender for transformation?

~ Where am I noticing and encountering God throughout my day?

~ In what situations have I witnessed the faithful work of my Creator?

Dearest God, my Creator and Friend,
I am grateful for the transformational work that you are doing in my life each and every day. Please help me to be open to your Spirit and trust in the journey. Soften my heart to receive the many graces that you offer so freely and allow me to recognize the need to rest in your loving arms in complete reliance on you. May I find beauty in my brokenness, trusting that you are transforming me.

In faith, I will journey with you by my side. Amen.

People are like stained glass windows. They sparkle and shine when the sun is out, but when darkness sets in, their beauty is revealed only if there is a light from within.
~Elizabeth Kubler-Ross

ELEVEN

LIGHT

*"The Lord is my light and my salvation—whom shall I fear? The Lord is the stronghold
of my life—of whom should I be afraid?"*
—Psalm 27:1

There are some seasons in our lives when darkness seems to shroud our ability to see clearly. In these times, our yearning for light and clarity challenges us, but it also has the potential to draw us closer to the one true light. As you begin to notice spaces of light, brightness, and hopeful moments, you are moving closer in your relationship with our Creator. Acknowledging His presence in the small ways He reaches out to you fosters joy, and as your focus shifts, darkness fades. His light is transforming you and guiding you to new opportunities.

As you remain open in mind, body, soul, and spirit, you can become a conduit of His light, reflecting His love and beauty into the world. Imagine the gentle flow of love traversing every cell in your body and radiating into the depths of your soul. The warmth, comfort, and security that His presence emits within you is like no other. Allow these images of His love and light to pervade your being as you breathe, and believe that you have captured the light of the world. You—yes, you—have been chosen to receive in abundance. Maybe the time in darkness is necessary for us to find gratitude in the beautiful light.

~How might you allow light into the darkness?

Dearest God, my Creator and Friend,
I am grateful for your endless light and love that flows so generously within my life.
I know you desire to share it freely with me regardless of my circumstances. Please
help me to notice your presence in my life and guide me to be all that you intended
me to be. May I remain open to you and become a conduit of your love and light so
that those around me will feel your presence when they are with me.
In faith, I will journey with you by my side. Amen.

Have patience with all things. But first of all with yourself.

~St. Francis de Sales

TWELVE

JOURNEY

"Trust in the Lord with all your heart and lean not on your own understanding; in all your ways submit to him, and he will make your paths straight."
—Proverbs 3:5–6

As you look ahead, your path may not always seem well-defined. Could it be that the blurriness is a sign to invite your Creator more deeply into the moment? Maybe the unseen along your journey is a beautiful gift awaiting you—a gift that is unimaginable and made just for you at just the right moment. He is never early, but rest assured, He is never later either!

Reframe your anxious thoughts to hopeful anticipation and allow your focus to shift to a peaceful presence. Breathe deeply and know that each step is guided by the One who created you and knows you intimately. Trust that He is with you. There will be times when you feel as if He is carrying you, and at others, you may feel as though you are skipping alongside Him in precious freedom and everything in between. No matter where you are, faith and trust are paramount in discovering each step of your journey.

~What seems blurry right now that I can surrender to my Creator?

Dearest God, my Creator and Friend,
I am grateful for your undivided attention in my life. It is hard for me to imagine how intricate your plans are for me. Please help me to trust in each step of my journey knowing that you are beside me every moment of the way. May I continue to grow in my faith and abide in your endless love and provision.
In faith, I will journey with you by my side. Amen.

THIRTEEN

TRUST

"For we walk by faith, not by sight."
—2 Corinthians 5:7

Have you experienced days where doubt comes in and takes a turn whispering in your ears? Moments where all our hope and courage are whisked away in one rushing swoop? How can we put a pause and eventual stop on those unhealthy thoughts that eat away at our dreams? Parking our minds and hearts in a deep trust for our Creator can be the antidote to the vicious limitations that doubt places upon us.

Sometimes, the more you cannot see, the more there may be that is yet to be revealed. The graces that await are so unbelievable that even a tiny glimpse would ruin the grandiose surprise. Our God is the Creator of unbelievable masterpieces. If you are ever in doubt, notice how He paints the sky over and over, never becoming weary of making something new. Believe that through His thoughtful transformation, He is bringing beauty from brokenness and transforming our messes into miracles. Lean into Him for the strength, grace, and love you need to move through each and every moment.

~What can I give to God that I've tried relentlessly to transform without success?

Dearest God, my Creator and Friend,
I am grateful for your patience with me as I turn from doubt and look to you. Please help me to trust in your plans knowing that your strength will always sustain me. Guide me in the moments where I am dim with doubt and need to be transformed in my faith. May I be rooted in a deep reliance upon you for all that I need because you are my provider, my strength, and my refuge.
In faith, I will journey with you by my side. Amen.

In prayer, sometimes we expect too much of ourselves and too little of God.

~Catherine Goodman Farley

FOURTEEN

MERCY

"He saved us, not because of the righteous things we had done,
but because of his mercy. He saved us though the washing of rebirth and renewal
by the Holy Spirit."
—Titus 3:5

Our Creator knew that we would sin and be broken throughout our earthly journeys. This is why His mercy is so abundant and always available. It's not something we earn or deposit, save or spend. No, God's mercy is free to each and every one of us. He wants us to turn to Him and receive this divine love and mercy that covers all the cracks and crevices we create with our humanly errors. Don't believe that you are not worthy or deserving of such a tremendous gift; you are!

Be open in your communication with your Creator about your challenges, your deepest wounds, and your pressing pains. He knows you intimately and loves when you turn to Him and share your heart and soul. He is a master at turning our wounds into wisdom, our pain into purpose, and our brokenness into beauty. The miracle of mercy awaits.

~What sin, wound, or pain can I share with God today?

Dearest God, my Creator and Friend,
I am grateful for the endless mercy that flows from you. Please help me to turn to you and allow my sin, wounds, and pains to be transformed through your unconditional love for me. When my heart is broken open, heal me with your divine touch. When I feel weak and tired from my challenges, hold me with your strong and merciful arms. May I be comforted by your presence in my life.
In faith, I will journey with you by my side. Amen.

Comparison is the thief of joy.

~C. S. Lewis

FIFTEEN

GRATITUDE

"For where your treasure is, there your heart will be also."
—Matthew 6:21

Focusing on our gifts brings forth an attitude of gratitude, ultimately releasing us from feelings of inadequacy and comparison. When we notice the many God-given talents and graces that He shares with us, our hearts become full. In these moments of realization, you can feel your heart being moved closer to your Creator. He created us to be loved deeply, and it is through this mutual admiration that we begin to understand the breadth of His love.

As you are open to the fullness of His love flowing into your heart, imagine how this abundance can be shared with those around you. Turning your heart to gratitude and the fullness of God's love transforms you, and in turn, it brings about a ripple effect within your circle of influence. With the opening and focus of one heart to our Creator, abundant love flows and rises within many.

~How can I be the catalyst and conduit of unconditional love?

Dearest God, my Creator and Friend,
I am grateful for the many gifts that you have given me. Please help me to focus on my uniqueness and the unconditional love you share with me. Guide me to turn to you in moments when I begin to compare or feel inadequate, knowing that you will equip me for where I am called to serve you. May I be a catalyst and conduit for love in all that I encounter.
In faith, I will journey with you by my side. Amen.

SIXTEEN

PATIENCE

"You do not realize what I am doing, but later you will understand."
—John 13:7

Exploring the Latin root of words often provides greater depth and understanding. In the case of "patience," we are brought to the root, "pati," which means to suffer. When we think of suffering, we imagine hardship, pain, and unwanted circumstances, but what if suffering is the root of something new and beautiful trying to break out of the old and worn? Could we patiently walk through a season of transformation if we knew that something new could spring forth?

Placing our trust in things not seen and in the sometimes slow work of our Creator challenges us. However, often patience can be one of our best instructors, providing a shift in perspective, a present-focused mentality, and an openness for potential and possibility that we never imagined. In a society where reliance and rest seem counterintuitive, the way of our Creator is to rely on those virtues for His most glorious work. As you let go and let God transform your mind, body, soul, and spirit, trust that every moment has meaning. He is the God of intricate detail, and intricacy takes time.

~What do I have difficulty comprehending in this season of my life?

Dearest God, my Creator and Friend,
I am grateful for your great care, concern, and love for every detail of my life. Please help me to rest and relax, trusting that you have all the intricate details arranged just for me. Allow me to relinquish my worries and know that your timing is always best. May I believe that you are transforming me into the person that you intended me to be and that the making of a masterpiece takes time.
In faith, I will journey with you by my side. Amen.

Meaningful change is a process.

~Brené Brown

SEVENTEEN

PERSEVERANCE

"With God all things are possible."
—Matthew 19:26

Prayer and perseverance go hand in hand. As you spend time with God, His presence catalyzes an unbelievable peace and divine strength that helps you to move forward in hope. Sometimes, a simple glance upward provides the reassurance that you are not alone, and other days, time sitting in silence being held by your Creator is needed. Begin to notice how you can commune with your Creator. He will meet you where you are; just ask Him.

Once you explore your unique ways to pray and connect with God, begin to weave these moments into your days. A new rhythm will evolve, and you will notice that you are growing in faith and believing in your dreams. Often, God is the one who places incredible dreams upon your heart. Perseverance with God's help will make them possible. Believe that He is with you and is transforming you to be the most amazing version of you!

~What daily practice of prayer or rhythm of communing with God is drawing me closer to Him?

Dearest God, my Creator and Friend,
I am grateful for the many ways I have discovered to connect with you.
Please help me to notice your presence as I go through my days and give me the strength, peace, and hope to persevere in the amazing and challenging seasons of my life. May I be transformed into the beautiful person that you intended me to be with love at the center of all that I do.
In faith, I will journey with you by my side. Amen.

Once you choose hope, anything is possible.

~Christopher Reeve

EIGHTEEN

HOPE

"Not only so, but we also glory in our sufferings, because we know that suffering produces perseverance; perseverance, character; and character, hope. And hope does not put us to shame, because God's love has been poured out into our hearts through the Holy Spirit, who has been given to us."
—Romans 5:3-5

Suffering is hard, and it's even harder to comprehend that beauty can blossom from our challenges. Scripture reassures us that deep hope can be found in the midst of the messes in our lives when we praise God and allow Him to transform our tough situations into character-building moments.

Believe that you can thrive amid the messy when you focus on the beauty that can spring forth from the brokenness that our earthly existence permits. Noticing the progress that you make spiritually is a reaffirming way to see your growth. Maybe your doubts are beginning to wane, your fears seem to be less invasive, or your heart has been moved to hold less resentfulness or regret. This is transformative growth that is healing your mind, body, soul, and spirit. You are progressing in your relationship with your Creator, and His love always prevails.

~What challenges in my life are beginning to seem more hopeful?

Dearest God, my Creator and Friend,
I am grateful for the deep hope in my soul that only you can provide. Please give me the strength and grace to navigate the messes in my life. Continue to transform my brokenness into beauty so that I may see the fruits of your love. Even though it is hard to suffer, help me to embrace it and walk through it for your glory.
In faith, I will journey with you by my side. Amen.

NINETEEN

GRACE

"My grace is sufficient for you, for my power is made perfect in weakness."
—2 Corinthians 12:9

Grace is a gift from God given abundantly without measure or earning. Plain and simple, God desires for us to receive His abundant graces of love and mercy every moment of every day, rain or shine, in sin and sickness, and in joy or suffering. That is just how God works. He loves each and every one of His children so much that He showers grace upon us without reserve.

God intended us to have weaknesses because without them, we wouldn't need the tremendous gift of grace. As we grow in our faith journey with God, grace transforms us. It gives us the power to forgive, to love deeply, and to reflect these beautiful gifts to those in our lives. When we expand our openness to the work of our Creator, His Spirit moves within us to stir this beauty that is ultimately what we share in the world.

~Where are you noticing God's grace transforming you?

Dearest God, my Creator and Friend,
I am grateful for your abundant grace that flows upon me. Please help me to be
open to this amazing gift and notice the many ways your grace is present in my life.
May I share this overflowing grace of love and mercy with all those I encounter.
In faith, I will journey with you by my side. Amen.

"Nothing ever happens in the world that does not happen first inside human hearts."

-Fulton Sheen

TWENTY

ABUNDANCE

"The thief comes only to steal and kill and destroy;
I came that they may have life, and have it to the full."
—John 10:10

God brings forth abundance in life, not necessarily in the material sense, but more so in the spiritual and soulful manner. As you are open to His Spirit, you will begin to see the fruits of peace, love, joy, patience, kindness, goodness, faithfulness, gentleness, and self-control blossoming in your life. Each one of these beautiful gifts is yours to keep, as they are what truly makes life vibrant.

At times, these fruits feel elusive and unreachable, but those are the moments when we need to look deeply at what we have placed in our hearts and souls that may be taking up the space where the Spirit can dwell. As C. S. Lewis once shared, "Comparison is the thief of joy." Your spiritual abundance is unique to you. God knows exactly which fruits you are lacking, so allow Him to fill you with them. His fullness feels so amazing.

~Which fruits of the Spirit do I deeply desire?

Dearest God, my Creator and Friend,
I am grateful for the transformation of my mind, body, soul, and spirit that you are providing. Although it can feel painful at times, I trust that you are creating sustainable beauty within me. Please help me to keep my heart and soul open to you and bring the Spirit and all of your fruits upon me. Give me abundant life in communion with you.
In faith, I will journey with you by my side. Amen.

THOUGHTS

TO PONDER

INTRODUCTION TO INTEGRATION

"Because of the Lord's great love we are not consumed, for his compassions never fail. They are new every morning; great is your faithfulness."
—Lamentations 3:22–23

As you embrace new rhythms and can reframe your thoughts in the light of God's word, worldly challenges will fade from your focus. You are beginning to live more freely, noticing God's presence throughout your days and trusting that He is at work especially in the unseen. Pain has percolated to the surface, and you have practiced releasing it into God's healing hands. When fear and doubt begin swirling about, you are turning to God's promises to strengthen and empower you.

Your mind is being renewed and so will follow your emotion. You no longer have to ride the roller coaster. God brings truth, fostering hope, love, joy, and life contrary to the undermining work of the evil one who loves to see us stay in places of despair, confusion, and chaos. Rest in the hands of your Creator and allow Him to empower you to view your discomfort as a place to ask for grace—a grace that will replace your pain with purpose. Recall that it is what we do with our pains and worries that paves our path for healing.

As you journey the next ten days, focus on the word and scripture each day, inviting God to continue to weave His truth into your mind, body, soul, and spirit. Go back to your sacred place (an enveloping chair, a special spot outdoors, or a religious location) and be present with your Creator. Ponder these questions and allow His Spirit to renew and affirm you. He is the greatest physician and can mend every pain and wound imaginable. Breathe deeply and believe in your potential.

TO PONDER . . .

~ Which Bible verse or word has resonated deeply within me?

~ Where am I seeing peace, joy, and hope come alive in my life?

~ Where are some of my sacred spots? How can I incorporate them into the rhythm of each day?

Dearest God, my Creator and Friend,
I am grateful for your open arms, your healing touch, and your love for me. Your light is illuminating my path as I renew my mind, body, soul, and spirit. Please help me to continue to trust and notice the many ways you care for me each and every day. May I hold fast to faith and confidently expect your peace and love to heal me. In faith, I will journey with you by my side. Amen.

When the voice of God speaks to you, it comes with courage, conviction, and peace.
~Catherine Goodman Farley

TWENTY-ONE

BELIEVE

"I do believe; help me overcome my unbelief!"
—Mark 9:24

Our belief system is foundational in our lives. When uncertainty arises, insecurities may mount, and your stability may feel challenged. Holding tight to what you know to be true is reaffirming. The truth is that the Spirit of God is alive and dwells within you at all times, ready to secure you in your faith and guide you as you step out into the unknown. Believe it and rely upon Him.

As you welcome the Spirit into your mind, body, soul, and spirit, you will notice a sense of comfort with the unseen. Moving forward into undiscovered territory may begin to excite you. The unknowns and uncertainties are becoming a place for curiosity and adventure, a space to explore the deeper you and connect with tremendous meaning in your life. You are being transformed from the inside by your Creator, moving forward in healing, and being your best "you," exactly who you were created to be.

~Where am I finding joy that I didn't have before?

Dearest God, my Creator and Friend,
I am grateful for your Spirit that inspires, guides, and brings forth the most beautiful me. Please help me to continue to be open to Him, notice His nudges, and follow His prompts. Bring healing to the wounds in my mind, body, and soul, and allow me to recognize the beauty in each and every one of my cracks. May I trust that transformation in your hands will bring true peace, joy, and love.
In faith, I will journey with you by my side. Amen.

Joy is the holy fire that keeps our purpose warm and our intelligence aglow.

~Helen Keller

TWENTY-TWO

JOY

"May the God of hope fill you with all joy and peace as you trust in him, so that you may overflow with hope by the power of the Holy Spirit."
—Romans 15:13

Understanding the difference between happiness and joy is essential in our spiritual growth. Happiness is linked to situations and circumstances, but deep joy is determined by our relationship with our Creator. No matter what pain or hardship you may face, you can find joy and peace. The power of the Spirit dwells within you and empowers you to traverse challenging experiences that derail earthly happiness.

Spiritual joy and peace are deeply rooted in your soul as you relate to your Creator and place your trust and hope in Him. In challenging times, invite the Spirit to move fervently in your life. His powerful presence and dwelling within you brings forth true joy and peace no matter your circumstances. As you breathe, imagine breathing in the Spirit of peace and joy and breathing out any worry and anxiety. Integrating the Spirit of your Creator into tough moments will bring you unexpected graces to move forward along a path intended just for you. This is the path to becoming exactly who your Creator intended you to be.

~Where do I see the Holy Spirit, my Advocate, guiding me?

Dearest God, my Creator and Friend,
I am grateful for you sending your Spirit to dwell within me. Please help me notice His nudges, prompts, and guidance as I trust in your presence in my life. Give me strength to take each breath with hope in you and the work you are doing in my life to heal me. May I notice the small moments of joy and savor the deep peace that a relationship with you provides.
In faith, I will journey with you by my side. Amen.

TWENTY-THREE

HEALING

"Jesus reached out his hand and touched the man. 'I am willing,' he said. 'Be clean!' And immediately the leprosy left him."
—Luke 5:13

As you invite the Spirit of God into your life, you may begin to notice areas that feel uncomfortable. There may be a stirring in your soul or a restlessness in your heart. When we are still and notice these indicators in our bodies, we are made aware that transformation is taking place. Maybe pain from sin has taken root and needs to be lifted up for forgiveness. Sin and its' wounds can take up beautiful space that was intended for the living Spirit of God to dwell. Asking for forgiveness of our sins allows guilt, shame, and heavy burdens to begin to break apart, yielding to the abundant love and mercy that conquers them.

The Spirit transforms our shame into strength, our guilt into courage, and our burdens into hope. Known as our Advocate, the Spirit of our loving God wants to lead us to a fruitful life, one in which we thrive. It doesn't mean that we will have lives free of pain or hurt, but it does mean that our wounds can be covered with the healing love and mercy of our Creator. Embracing a rhythm of surrender and being present to Him will bring about a beautifully wholesome way to journey through the peaks and valleys that our lives behold.

~What sin is rooted in my heart and soul that can be surrendered and forgiven?

Dearest God, my Creator and Friend,
I am grateful for the many ways that you reach out to me. Please help me to notice when sin is taking root in my heart and soul. As my wounds are healed in your gentle hands, transform my mind, body, and soul to reflect your love. May my heart and soul be filled with the abundant graces of your living presence.
In faith, I will journey with you by my side. Amen.

I am a little pencil in the hands of a writing God who is
sending a love letter to the world.
~Saint Mother Teresa

TWENTY-FOUR

LOVE

"Above all else, guard your heart, for everything you do flows from it."
—Proverbs 4:23

Our hearts can be a source of tremendous wisdom when we allow the Spirit to dwell with us. As the loving and gentle Spirit resides within you, you are able to grow in unimaginable ways. You will begin noticing "God winks" all around you. These moments are created just for you, affirming that you are His beloved. Walking in His presence, you sense His whisper encouraging you and leading you to places you may have never imagined.

The transformation that is occurring brings about a deep and abiding love that cannot be created by your own will. As the love grows stronger, allow it to flow freely within you, into every part of your mind, body, soul, and spirit. Take a moment to visualize every cell within you filled with this unconditional love. You are becoming an effective conduit of the love that God intends for you to bring into the world. Continue to stay open to this gift. It is yours to savor and share.

~Where am I noticing the warmth and love of God within my body?

Dearest God, my Creator and Friend,
I am grateful for your unconditional love that you share abundantly with me. Please send your Spirit into the places of my mind, body, heart, and soul that feel broken and need your loving balm. I have faith and trust that you are transforming me to be a reflection of your love. Help me to be open and courageous so I may be a beautiful wellspring of life. I know I was created to thrive with you as my guide.
In faith, I will journey with you by my side. Amen.

Adopt the pace of nature: her secret is patience.

~Ralph Waldo Emerson

TWENTY-FIVE

AWE

"There is no fear in love. But perfect love drives out fear, because fear has to do with punishment. The one who fears is not made perfect in love."
—1 John 4:18

God desires to awe us with His presence in our lives. As you continue to invite the Holy Spirit to dwell within your mind, body, soul, and spirit, your fears and worries will be transformed to faith and hope. When you remain hopeful despite troubling circumstances, that is the awe-inspiring presence of God. Bring Him into the midst of the mess and unimaginable beauty will come forth.

As you place your trust in Him, you begin to understand how "perfect" His place of rest, of peace, and of presence truly is. Imagine His gentle hands wrapped around you, supporting you and shaping you for all that He has in store for His beloved. Rest your mind, body, soul, and spirit in this place of perfect care. You are His and He is in control. Fear is no longer a part of you.

~What is one fear that you can release to your loving Creator?

Dearest God, my Creator and Friend,
I am grateful for your constant presence in my life. Please help me to release my fears into your loving hands and trust that you are holding me tightly. Help me to be awed many moments in my days. May I shift my focus to you and the abundant love you provide, knowing that true joy and hope is found in your presence.
In faith, I will journey with you by my side. Amen.

TWENTY-SIX

SUPPORT

"So do not fear, for I am with you; do not be dismayed, for I am your God. I will strengthen you and help you; I will uphold you with my righteous right hand."
—Isaiah 41:10

As you continue to let go of the fears that may grip you, you will notice courage and strength growing. Moments that used to overwhelm you are now surmountable with the help of your Advocate, the Spirit. You are empowered to step further into the unknown, exploring possibilities that used to appear daunting. With fear fading, you have more space within your mind, body, soul, and spirit for love and potential to dwell. From these places, a renewed sense of being and life is evolving.

Allow your body to relax and focus on the rhythm of your breath. Take a slow deep breath, breathing in peace and potential. Envision that Spirit-infused air moving throughout your body into every cell. Each of those cells is replicating and building a beautiful foundation within your being. You are firmly rooted in God's love, and His strength and peace are multiplying within you. Your potential is expanding beyond your imagination.

~Where in your body do you physically feel the energy of the Holy Spirit?

Dearest God, my Creator and Friend,
I am grateful for your Spirit and the transformation that you are bringing to fruition in me. Please continue to guide me as I surrender my mind, body, soul, and spirit to your care. Help me to notice the changes and begin to see the beautiful potential within me. May I grow in your love and be a conduit of the many graces you freely provide.

In faith, I will journey with you by my side. Amen.

When we offer our whole selves to God, He takes our wounds and creates something beautiful.

~Elza Spaedy

TWENTY-SEVEN

FREEDOM

"Now the Lord is the Spirit, and where the Spirit of the Lord is, there is freedom."
—2 Corinthians 3:17

With renewed inspiration from the Spirit of our loving Creator, you may begin to notice an awareness of self and novel interest in your surroundings. The world begins to look different when seen through the lens of the Spirit. You may find wonder in nature that you never experienced before or a stronger desire to serve others in a unique way as you grow more attuned to the nudges of the Spirit. As you follow His prompts, you feel a freedom to live boldly.

When past wounds and pains are restored through the love and care of God, your mind, body, soul, and spirit are reinvigorated with life. You may begin to feel affirmed in beliefs that you held prior to an unfortunate life circumstance, or you may begin to hold new beliefs surrounding your God-given potential. Whatever the case, trust that your "I AM" is an amazingly unique foundation for you to move forward in faith.

⁓What are three "I AM" statements that you are beholding today?
Examples: I AM courageous. I AM loved. I AM creative.

Dearest God, my Creator and Friend,
I am grateful for the freedom that can be found when I intentionally welcome the Holy Spirit into my life. Please help me continue to be open to your transformation and allow my mind, body, soul, and spirit to be molded into a beautiful reflection of you. May I become all that you intended for me to be and behold my unique I AMs with great courage.
In faith, I will journey with you by my side. Amen.

Make me a channel of your peace,
Where there is hatred let me bring your love,
Where there is injury your pardon Lord,
And where there's doubt true faith in you.

Make me a channel of your peace,
Where there's despair in life, let me bring hope,
Where there is darkness, only light,
And where there's sadness, ever joy.

O Master grant that I may never seek,
So much to be consoled as to console,
To be understood as to understand,
To be loved as to love with all my soul.

Make me a channel of your peace,
It is in pardoning that we are pardoned,
In giving of ourselves that we receive.
And in dying that we are born to eternal life.

-Saint Francis of Assisi

TWENTY-EIGHT

PEACE

"Finally, brothers and sisters, whatever is true, whatever is noble, whatever is right, whatever is pure, whatever is lovely, whatever is admirable, if anything is excellent or praiseworthy, think about such things. What you have learned or received or heard from me, put it into practice. And the God of peace will be with you."
—Philippians 4:8–9

As your affirmations of who you are in the image and likeness of your Creator take root, you will find your thoughts migrating to places of positivity. The truth of who you truly are as a beloved child of God is being woven into your being. When moments of doubt creep into your mind, acknowledge the thought for what it is and reframe to the truth of who you are. Repeating your I AMs replaces any ruminating thoughts that do not serve you.

Allow glimmering thoughts to replace negative triggers. As your mind is illuminated with truth, so your body follows. Imagine what the warm light of Christ can do. He brings beauty from brokenness, miracles from mess, and purpose from pain. Trust that He has brought the lovely, the gracious, and the beautiful into your life. You are connecting with it and bringing it forth in new ways.

~What truth am I noticing in my mind that wasn't there before?

Dearest God, my Creator and Friend,
I am grateful for the many graces that you bestow upon me. Please shine your light upon the truth and let it be my guide. As you illuminate my path, help me to walk in peace with complete surrender and trust in you. May the Spirit give me bold courage to share you with those I encounter each day.
In faith, I will journey with you by my side. Amen.

TWENTY-NINE

ENDURANCE

"Count it pure joy, my brothers and sisters, whenever you face trials of many kinds, because you know that testing of your faith produces perseverance. Let perseverance finish its work so that you may be mature and complete, not lacking in anything."
—James 1:2–4

When the Spirit is integrated into our lives, we are equipped and empowered to navigate any circumstances that may arise. You may notice that some of your most tremendous growth has occurred during your most challenging seasons. Through these times, we lean into our faith and God provides a supernatural strength that is not humanly achievable. We learn that taking one step at a time in trust and hope allows us to steady ourselves, stay balanced, and navigate obstacles that arise.

You may be amazed at your steady calm amid the peaks and valleys. No matter what you are traversing, the Spirit of your loving Creator is with you, supporting, advocating, and guiding you. As you open space in your mind, body, soul, and spirit, it will be filled completely and overflow with abundant graces. Recall that you are a conduit and be intentional with how the graces you receive may be shared.

~Where have you been able to share grace lately?

Dearest God, my Creator and Friend,
I am grateful for your presence in my life. I know that you are with me in the joyful moments and in my suffering. I praise you for your steady hand guiding and holding me. Help me to notice the graces that you bestow upon me and share them selflessly with others. May I be a reflection of your love in the world in all I say and do.
In faith, I will journey with you by my side. Amen.

What we look for is what we will see. What we see determines our perspective.
And our perspective becomes our reality.

~Lysa TerKeurst

THIRTY

RENEWAL

"Then your light will break forth like the dawn, and your healing will quickly appear;
then your righteousness will go before you, and the glory of the
Lord will be your rear guard."
—Isaiah 58:8

Each and every day is a new and fresh opportunity to grow and become. Some days will feel stagnant, while others may feel like you are clicking along with fervor that is beyond belief. Embrace each day and know that the same God and the same Spirit with the same love for you is present and working on your behalf. When He lives within you, you live beyond your capacity and your reach has a masterful extension.

As you are renewed, a beautiful ripple effect transmits to those around you. God brings new people, experiences, and connections into your midst that lift, inspire, and grow with you. He is the master at weaving a tapestry that is creative beyond our belief. Open your mind, body, soul, and spirit to His presence and watch the beauty blossom in your life. You are transformed and renewed in Him.

~What new experiences or connections are you noticing in your life?

Dearest God, my Creator and Friend,
I am grateful for fresh beginnings and the excitement they bring. Please help me to notice the many gifts that you bring into my life. Guide me to what is most important in your eyes and give me the courage to say yes to you. May I live as an authentic believer and reflect that all things come together for the glory of God.
In faith, I will journey with you by my side. Amen.

THOUGHTS

TO PONDER

INTRODUCTION TO AFFIRMATION

"Jesus turned and saw her. 'Take heart, daughter,' he said, 'your faith has healed you.'
And the woman was healed at that moment."
—Matthew 9:22

You are uniquely made and have experienced many moments that have molded you into the beautifully unique individual that you are. As you have placed your circumstances into the hands of your Creator, you may be noticing the new and unexpected evolving. You have been open to the work of the Spirit throughout this journey. Transformation and renewal are becoming part of your rhythm of life, and hopefully, you have a deeper sense of peace and joy. With the energy of the Spirit dwelling within you, you are reinvigorated and feel purposeful.

When we live lives that are intentional and filled with purpose, we not only feel fulfilled, but we also are most likely positively impacting those around us in profound ways. This is the work of our masterful Creator connecting us in community, weaving a tapestry of life filled with promise and potential. What may have felt ordinary becomes extraordinary in the hands of God. As Helen Keller once shared, "The best and most beautiful things in this world cannot be seen or even heard, but must be felt with the heart."

Moving forward into these last ten days, continue to focus on the word and scripture each day. As you invite the Spirit to dwell deeper in your mind, body, soul, and spirit, envision His loving presence within you, guiding you to be the most beautiful you. Ponder these questions and allow His thoughts to settle into your being. Thoughts of peace, hope, and purpose are yours to claim.

TO PONDER . . .

*~ What new rhythms have you embraced that are helping your
mind, body, soul, and spirit?*

~ Are there any relationships that are more engaging or fulfilling right now?

~ In what part of your body do you notice more peace and calm?

~ Is there a Bible verse, intention, or word of inspiration that is resonating with you?

Dearest God, my Creator and Friend,
I am grateful for this time I can spend with you and all that I have discovered. Help me to let go of thoughts that do not serve you. Fill me with your loving presence and illuminate my deepest and most unique gifts. Bring forth affirmation in my purpose and give me the courage to live intentionally sharing my gifts with those around me.

In faith, I will journey with you by my side. Amen.

The meaning of life is to find your gift. The purpose of life is to give it away.

~Pablo Picasso

THIRTY-ONE

DISCOVER

"And we know that in all things God works for the good of those who love him, who have been called according to his purpose."
—Romans 8:28

Being led by the Spirit, you are discovering possibilities that you may have never imagined. As you move forward, letting go of fears and doubt-filled thoughts, you are free to believe in your unlimited potential. Noticing the community of people around you, you may feel confident to share your God-given talents, desires, and hopes for the days to come. In sharing, you may notice that you are already surrounded by an army of "human angels" willing to support, encourage, and pray with you. Lean into community and lift one another to be all that God intended.

Each day becomes a new adventure as unique connections evolve and your most authentic self is affirmed. The joy that bubbles up is a beautiful energy rooted in your mind, body, soul, and spirit that is undeniably supernatural and a gift from God. Savor and share it as it flows abundantly in your life. For in sharing, community evolves where love and joy can multiply.

~Who brings joy and positive energy into your life?

Dearest God, my Creator and Friend,
I am grateful for your presence in my life as I discover more meaning and purpose each and every day. Please help me to continue to leave doubt on the doorstep and walk in confident faith knowing that you have a beautiful plan for my life. Keep me grounded in your love so that I may be the catalyst for community rooted in you. May I always notice your tender touches in my life.
In faith, I will journey with you by my side. Amen.

One touch of nature makes the whole world kin.

~William Shakespeare

THIRTY-TWO

WISDOM

"If any of you lacks wisdom, you should ask God, who gives generously to all without finding fault, and it will be given to you."
—James 1:5

Growth in your relationship with your Creator brings about tremendous wisdom and insight. As you look retrospectively, you begin to recognize how God was at work in many moments in your life weaving together the most glorious plan even amid challenging and painful seasons. The gift of wisdom comes with experience, relationship, and communication with our Creator. He can bring forth unimaginable insight when we pay attention to His prompts.

Through wisdom, we are learning, growing, and building a stronger foundation in our lives. Imagine a healthy live oak tree with its tremendous trunk, far-reaching limbs, and abundant green leaves. There are bends in the branches, chips in the bark, and even broken limbs at times, but the whole oak represents grounding, growth, and life. You are filled with this same resilience, strength, and wisdom brought about by a variety of seasons in your life. Hold these truths within your mind, body, soul, and spirit, believing that there is purpose in all you experience.

~What wisdom can you bring forth from a memorable season in your life?

Dearest God, my Creator and Friend,
I am grateful for the tremendous wisdom that you provide for me. Please help me to attend to your insight and grow in grace and virtue. Bring forth the fruits of love, joy, peace, patience, kindness, goodness, faithfulness, gentleness, and self-control in my life and in the lives of those around me. May the Spirit be alive and renew me to thrive.

In faith, I will journey with you by my side. Amen.

THIRTY-THREE

GIFTS

*"Therefore, if anyone is in Christ, the new creation has
come: The old has gone, the new is here!"*
—2 Corinthians 5:17

God is a generous giver, continuously providing for you. He wants to usher in fullness of life each and every day and does so in the most creative ways. As He masterfully weaves and gently molds with intricate care, rest assured that He will create more beauty than you could ever imagine. Continue to open your mind, body, soul, and spirit to the gifts that He is bestowing upon you.

You will experience moments when you are receiving and times when you are giving. Finding the balance of this beautiful exchange may require some reflection. You may be one who more easily receives, or maybe you tend to give until you are empty. If you notice an imbalance, take care to correct it. Imagine being a conduit of this gentle flow and exchange of gifts. Continue to hold a posture with your heart and palms of your hands open to your Creator who loves and gives unconditionally.

⁓What gifts are you receiving and/or giving right now?

Dearest God, my Creator and Friend,
I am grateful for the amazing graces that you bestow upon me each and every day. Your glorious imagination is greater than any gift I could conceive. Please help me to live uninhibited by earthly fears and concerns and to place my mind, body, soul, and spirit into your loving hands. As I hear your gentle voice and feel the movement of your Spirit, give me the strength I need to follow your way—a way of truth, of love, and of hope.

In faith, I will journey with you by my side. Amen.

Laugh often . . . laughter is a bubbly effervescent form of holiness.

~Anne Lamott

THIRTY-FOUR

SPIRITED

"Praise the Lord, my soul; all my inmost being, praise his holy name. Praise the Lord, my soul, and forget not all his benefits, who forgives all your sins and heals all your diseases, who redeems your life from the pit and crowns you with love and compassion, who satisfies your desires with good things so that your youth is renewed like the eagle's."
—Psalm 103:1-5

The boundless gift of the Spirit dwelling within us brings forth new freedom and is often the catalyst for novel inspiration. When you begin to sense this gentle stirring in your mind, body, and soul, pay attention with curiosity. Unleash your imagination and believe in the possibilities that are surfacing. God may be providing an opportunity to overcome an obstacle that has seemingly limited you. Follow the guideposts step by step in faith, knowing that His plans are glorious and have unlimited potential.

As you rise to this new dawn, you notice the vast horizon and feel a sense of deep awe. Your kinship with your Creator and the movement of His Spirit within you are teaching you to view your life from their perspective, one of fullness and unbelievable possibilities. Maybe your deepest, soul-rooted desires are beginning to sprout. Lean into your faith, commune with your Creator, and allow the growth to blossom.

~What new potential are you sensing in your mind, body, soul, or spirit?

Dearest God, my Creator and Friend,
I am so grateful for the strength you are giving me to trust and believe in my potential. I know that with you by my side, I am beloved and boundless. Please help me to grow in your love and to notice where you are working in my life to bring about a glorious dawn. Give me the deep faith I need to continue to walk with you and become the most beautiful version of me.
In faith, I will journey with you by my side. Amen.

Invite the Holy Spirit into every breath you take.
~Catherine Goodman Farley

THIRTY-FIVE

DISCIPLINE

"Do not conform to the pattern of this world, but be transformed by the renewing of your mind. Then you will be able to test and approve what God's will is—his good, pleasing and perfect will."
—Romans 12:2

Earthly temptations are real and present in our lives, but through the continuous transformation that the Spirit provides, we can reorient to our Creator at any moment. It is often a simple glance upward or a gentle whisper to Him asking for His guidance that shifts our focus. He knows our mind, body, soul, and spirit intimately and understands exactly what we need to move forward with beautiful intention. Following His directives is not a jarring, painful movement but a gentle step in faith and hope.

Maybe you are craving moments of stillness and reflection. Try beginning your day with some reading, writing or prayer, meditating and stretching, or time in nature exercising your body. Notice how your rhythms are shaping you and how they impact your mind, body, soul, and spirit. Being intentional with how you connect with your Creator will allow His beautiful intentions for you to flourish. He created you to thrive, and with His hands and His Spirit, you will.

~What ritual or rhythm is bringing you joy and fullness of life?

Dearest God, my Creator and Friend,
I am grateful for the renewal of my mind, body, soul, and spirit. Please help me to continue to be open to the beautiful transformation that you bring about in my life. Guide me in rhythms and disciplines that can be the catalyst for becoming who you intended me to be. May I notice where you are calling me and meet you there with hope in my beautiful potential.

In faith, I will journey with you by my side. Amen.

THIRTY-SIX

RISE

"Arise, shine, for your light has come, and the glory of the Lord rises upon you. See, darkness covers the earth and thick darkness is over the peoples, but the Lord rises upon you and his glory appears over you. Nations will come to your light, and the kings to the brightness of your dawn. Lift up your eyes and look about you."

—Isaiah 60:1–4

With each new day, a fresh opportunity is upon you to rise and meet your Creator and all that He has for you. You are enlightened and have come so far in your journey. As you continue to look to the light, you and your surroundings are illuminated. You may notice spaces in your surroundings that are dimmer than others. This may be where God is calling you to shine and bring your beautiful light.

Imagine God's aerial view of all of His Creation. He knows exactly where your tremendous gifts are needed and how this connection may, in turn, fill you. His light brings you new awareness and direction. Allow it to pervade your mind, body, soul, and spirit, fostering a deeper purpose that is uniquely you. When light pervades you, you reorient to what matters most. Rise and follow His call.

~What do you notice being illuminated in your surroundings?

Dearest God, my Creator and Friend,
I am grateful for the glorious light you bring into all of your Creation. Enlighten me with your love and guide me to where you are calling. Help me to have the courage to step out and be all that you intended me to be. May I be a beacon of hope and bring about a brightness that reflects you.

In faith, I will journey with you by my side. Amen.

Be who God meant you to be and you will set the world on fire.

~St. Catherine of Siena

THIRTY-SEVEN

POSSIBILITY

"For no word from God will ever fail."
—Luke 1:37

When potential is realized, impossibility fades from focus. You begin to view your life from the spiritual eyes of your heart and soul where God's desires and your desires commune. Moving forward in your purpose begins to seem more effortless and natural. Light and grace from your Creator have been the catalyst for believing in the newness of your life.

Each and every grace-filled step you take glorifies God. From the smiles you share to the positivity you spread in your vocation, your life is a song of praise and gratitude to your Creator. You are His unique masterpiece. The details only become more and more intricate when He places His artistic touch upon them. Continue to invite Him and watch the endless beauty unfold.

~What new possibility is before you?

Dearest God, my Creator and Friend,
I am so grateful for your masterful touch in my life. You have brought about a new perspective that brings me great joy and excitement. Please help me to notice the beautiful possibilities that you create. May my life glorify you and may I be all that you intended me to be.
In faith, I will journey with you by my side. Amen.

Don't ask what the world needs. Ask what makes you come alive and go do it.
Because what the world needs is people who have come alive.

~Howard Thurman

THIRTY-EIGHT

EMPOWERED

"I thank Christ Jesus our Lord, who has given me strength, that he considered me trustworthy, appointing me to his service."
—1 Timothy 1:12

Gratitude is empowering and often directs us to what is working and important in our lives. As you shift your focus to thanksgiving for what you do have in your life, thoughts of what you lack may fade. This free space in your mind, body, soul, and spirit is now open to the many graces that flow freely from God. Allow the grace to fill you, empowering you to bring forth your beautiful self into the world. You are desired, needed, and poised to make an impact.

C.S. Lewis aptly shared, "Comparison is the thief of joy." Each of us is uniquely called, providentially equipped, and perfectly created to thrive. Allowing God's vision to come to life in you brings about a deep joy, peace, and satisfaction that is truly supernatural. This is the power that only He possesses—a power that empowers you to become your beautiful you.

~What new strength is evolving within you?

Dearest God, my Creator and my Friend,
I am so grateful for your attention to detail in my life. You are empowering me to help bring about a beautiful purpose and mission. Help me to notice the nudges of your Spirit and follow the amazing path you have placed before me. May I walk with a deep joy and peace that can only come from you.
In faith, I will journey with you by my side. Amen.

THIRTY-NINE

MISSION

"You did not choose me, but I chose you and appointed you that you might go and bear fruit—fruit that will last—and so that whatever you ask in my name the Father will give you. This is my command: Love each other."
—John 15:16–17

You were created with a unique mission in mind. Just as God sent His Son, Jesus, to bring love and hope into a fallen world, you are called to this same purpose. The ways we fulfill this call look different, but our grounding in God's unconditional love is the same. It joins us together in community over the ages and brings forth the same fulfillment of the human spirit. That is the unchanging and consistent love of our Creator alive in us.

As you continue to receive God's abundant love, allow it to refresh and renew you, filling you with supernatural giftedness. The overflow of this love from your life will bring about tremendous, far-reaching fruits. Over time, you will notice the ripple effect building and the loving impact you have had on others flowing back to you. The beautiful circle of life that your Creator intended is prospering and His kingdom is well. This is the glorious culmination of your "yes" and your openness to His love. Mission complete.

~Where have you noticed the ripple effect of God's love in your surroundings?

Dearest God, my Creator and Friend,
I am so grateful for the gift of your Son, Jesus, who taught an earthly way to share love and hope. Please guide me as I fulfill your mission for me. Help me to reflect you in all that I say and do. May my loving mission on earth please and glorify you.
In faith, I will journey with you by my side. Amen.

May the light of your soul guide you.

May the light of your soul bless your work

You do with the secret love and warmth of your heart.

May you see in what you do the beauty of your own soul.

May the sacredness of your work bring healing, light, and renewal to those who work

with you and to those who see and receive your work.

May work never weary you.

May it release within you wellsprings of refreshment, inspiration, and excitement.

May you be present in what you do.

May you never become lost in the bland absences.

May the day never burden you.

May dawn find you awake and alert, approaching your new day with dreams,

possibilities, and promises.

May evening find you gracious and fulfilled.

May you go into the night blessed, sheltered, and protected.

May your soul calm, console, and renew you.

~John O'Donohue

FORTY

DAWN

"See, I am doing a new thing! Now it springs up; do you not perceive it? I am making a way in the wilderness and streams in the wasteland."

—Isaiah 43:19

Life with the Spirit of our Creator paves a path where restoration, refreshment, and renewal are always available. He brings about transformation that heals our brokenness, change that shifts our focus to hope, and inspiration that enlivens us. As you've opened your mind, body, soul, and spirit to the beautiful work of your Creator, you may notice a new spark in your curiosity, courage, and resolve.

Receiving the many graces from above, you are being filled with supernatural peace, love, and joy. Allow these graces to flow through you into every part of your being. You are experiencing a deeper connection and a new horizon with limitless potential and opportunity. Clarity is yours as you see your life through the eyes of your Creator. He has been by your side in the desert, preparing this new dawn.

~What do you see on the horizon that you are ready to walk toward?

Dearest God, my Creator and Friend,
I am so grateful for the abundant graces I am receiving from spending time with you and your word. Help me to continue to recognize your gentle whisper and the prompts of your Spirit. As I look to the horizon, illuminate my path as I renew my faith in possibilities and purpose. May I lead a life filled with purpose that glorifies you.

In faith, I will journey with you by my side. Amen.

THOUGHTS

TO PONDER

AFTERWORD

"Now to Him who is able to do immeasurably more than all we ask or imagine, according to his power that is at work within us."
—Ephesians 3:20

My hope and prayer are that your forty-day journey from desert to dawn has deepened your connection with your Creator and His powerful Spirit, filling you with renewed hope. You courageously rose each day and opened your mind, body, soul, and spirit to the transformative work of our healing God. Through the words, scripture, questions, and prayers, you had the opportunity to ponder your life through the lens of your Creator. Maybe you noticed a place of brokenness that needed healing, a loneliness that needed a companion, or possibly a dark space that yearned for light. Whatever you needed, I hope that you felt God meet you there.

I commend you for surrendering to the stillness and carving out the time to reflect and grow. Discipline is required to bring new rhythms into your life, and you have done it. I encourage you to continue to set your sacred space, spend time in the presence of God, and call on the Spirit to renew and refresh you. Hopefully, you have discovered unexpected joy, abundant mercies, and wisdom that have been woven into your being. You were created with a beautifully unique purpose. You were created to thrive.

May you always notice God's loving whisper and the gentle nudges of His Spirit.

There is a divine current of grace running through this world connecting us to each other and healing us all.

~Kathy Izard

ACKNOWLEDGMENTS

Creating this devotional has been a journey for which I am incredibly grateful. To Julie Barnett, Kathy Brown, Kim Hall, and Maureen Osborne, thank you for your willingness to collaborate and share your amazing talents; to my dear friends and sisters in Christ, Katy Brame Erikson, Amy Byrnes, Margie Eades, Gina Fishburne, Connie Hawkins, Julie Hollar, Bridgett Bell Langson, Lynne Ray Masonis, Stacie Schreiner, Nicole Schrift, Elza Spaedy, Susan Walpole, Teddy Walpole, Katie Kibbe, Leslie McKillop, Holly Lanzas, Kathleen Cook and Marcie Elaasar your encouragement and support with this project means more than you will ever know; and to my faithful early readers, David Box, Mary Martha Felkner, Lauran Godwin, Deb Halliday, Amy Haskell, Kathy Izard, Bess Kercher, and Grace Slaton, your wisdom and insight is invaluable; and the root of it all—my family, my husband, Trey and our three children, Madeline, Mary Catherine, and James; my parents Mary and Myron Goodman; my inlaws, Jan and Jim Farley, and all of my extended family, Meg and Jason Summers, Jen and Myron Goodman, Julianne and Michael Goodman, Maria and Chris Goodman, Stephanie and John Farley, Ashley and Chase Kerley, and Matt Icard, thank you for walking beside me.

"Alone we can do so little; together we can do so much."

-Helen Keller

ABOUT THE AUTHOR

Catherine Goodman Farley believes every individual was created in the image and likeness of God and that He intends for each of us to thrive. As a practicing physical therapist with over twenty-four years of experience, she loves learning about the intricate connection of the mind, body, soul, and spirit. Her personal challenge in her early forties with severe anxiety, panic disorder, and PTSD was the catalyst for this inspiring collection of reflections. Through the merging of faith and science, Catherine discovered divine peace and healing and desires to share this hope with others. Catherine continues to grow in her spiritual life and shares her journey through her writing, speaking, and Well Women workshops.

She resides in Charlotte, North Carolina, with her husband and three children. Catherine is also the author of the Explore with Mimi children's book series.

www.catherinegoodmanfarley.com
www.explorewithmimi.com
IG @catherinegfarley
Facebook: Catherine Goodman Farley

ABOUT THE ARTIST

Julie Barnett rediscovered her love of art and painting after taking a leave of absence from her marketing career in order to raise her young children. She is primarily a self-taught intuitive artist but has also studied from a variety of accomplished artists. Julie strives to capture the unique beauty of subjects by using bright colors and expressive brushstrokes in landscape, still life and abstract paintings. Her works hang in homes and businesses across the US.

Born and raised in Dayton, Ohio, Julie graduated from the University of Cincinnati. She makes her home in Charlotte, North Carolina, with her husband and four sons.

www.juliebarnettfineart.com
IG @juliebarnettart

Made in United States
North Haven, CT
18 January 2022

14969499R00077